Bear's First Spanish Words

Clare Beaton

b small publishing
www.bsmall.co.uk

Plenty of lovely language-learning books for primary
school aged children are available from b small publishing.
Join us online for more information:
www.bsmall.co.uk
www.facebook.com/bsmallpublishing
@bsmallbear

b small publishing

Published by b small publishing ltd.
www.bsmall.co.uk
© b small publishing ltd. 2013

1 2 3 4 5

Printed in China by WKT Co. Ltd.

Editorial: Susan Martineau and Louise Millar
Design: Louise Millar
Production: Madeleine Ehm
Spanish adviser: María Concejo

ISBN 978-1-908164-68-1

British Library Cataloguing-in-Publication Data.
A catalogue record for this book is available from the British Library.

Índice
Contents

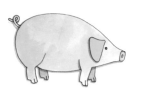

Los animales Animals

loss anee-mah-less

el gato

el gat-o

cat

el ratón

el rat-on

mouse

el caballo

el ka-bah-yo

horse

el perro

el peh-ro

dog

el pato

el pat-o

duck

la vaca

la bak-a

cow

el conejo

el kon-eh-ho

rabbit

la oveja

la obeh-ha

sheep

la gallina

la ga-yeen-a

chicken

10

la cabra
la kab-ra

goat

el cerdo
el thaird-o

pig

11

En casa At home

en <u>kah</u>-sa

la ventana

la ben<u>tah</u>-na

window

la puerta

la <u>pwair</u>ta

door

el frigorífico

el freego<u>ree</u>-feeko

fridge

la cama

la kah-ma

bed

la bañera

la banyair-a

bath

el reloj

el relokh

clock

La ropa Clothes

la ro-pa

el jersey

el hair-say

jumper

la falda

la fal-da

skirt

14

el vestido

el be<u>stee</u>do

dress

los zapatos

los tha<u>pat</u>-toss

shoes

la camiseta

la kah-mee-<u>seh</u>-ta

T-shirt

15

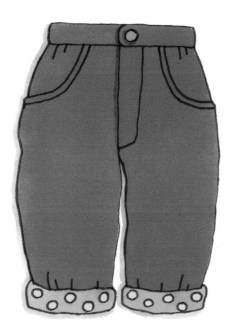

el pantalón
el panta<u>lon</u>

trousers

el sombrero

el som<u>brairo</u>

hat

los calcetines
loss kaltheh-<u>tee</u>-ness

socks

16

los pantalones cortos

loss panta-loness kor-toss

shorts

el pijama

el peehah-ma

pyjamas

el abrigo

el abree-go

coat

17

Los colores Colours

loss kol-<u>or</u>-ess

verde
<u>bair</u>-deh
green

rojo
<u>ro</u>-ho
red

18

rosa
rosa
pink

negro
naigro
black

blanco
blanko
white

gris
greess

grey

azul
ah-thool

blue

naranja
nah-ran-ha

orange

20

amarillo

ama<u>ree</u>-yo

yellow

brown

morado

mo<u>rah</u>-do

purple

21

La familia Family
la fam-eel-ya

la madre
la mah-dreh

mother

el padre
el pah-dreh

father

22

el abuelo
el abweh-lo
grandfather

la abuela
la abweh-la
grandmother

el hermano
el airmah-no
brother

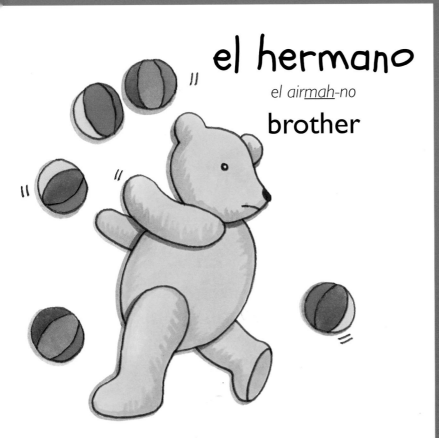

la hermana
la airmah-na
sister

23

La comida Food
la ko-<u>mee</u>-da

el pan
el pan

bread

la fruta
la <u>froo</u>-ta

fruit

el huevo
el way-bo

egg

el helado
el el-ah-doh

ice-cream

la leche
la leh-cheh

milk

el queso
el keh-soh

cheese

Los números Numbers

1 uno
oono
one

2 dos
doss
two

3 tres
tray-ss
three

4 cuatro
kwat-ro
four

5 cinco
think-o
five

6 seis
say-ss
six

27

7 siete

see-<u>eh</u>-teh

seven

8 ocho

<u>ocho</u>

eight

9 nueve
noo-eh-beh

nine

10 diez
dee-eth

ten

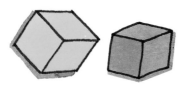

Los juguetes Toys
loss hoogait-ess

la pelota
la peh-lot-a

ball

el triciclo
el tree-thee-klo

tricycle

las piezas
lass pee-eh-thass

blocks

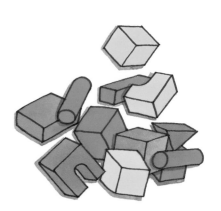

el tambor

el tam<u>bor</u>

drum

el rompecabezas

el rompeh-ka<u>beth</u>-ass

jigsaw puzzle

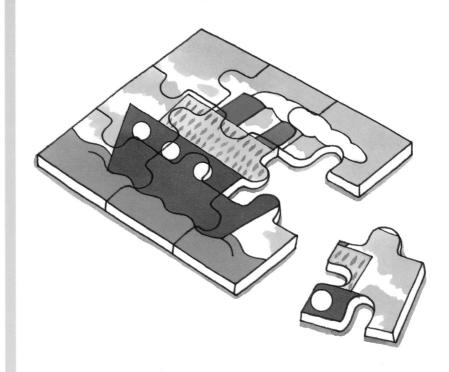

los lápices de colores

loss <u>lap</u>-eethess deh kol-<u>or</u>-ess

crayons

El transporte Transport

el transport-eh

la bicicleta
la bee-thee-klet-a
bicycle

la moto
la moh-toh
motorbike

el autobús
el ah-oto-boos
bus

el coche

el <u>ko</u>cheh

car

el avión

el abee-<u>on</u>

aeroplane

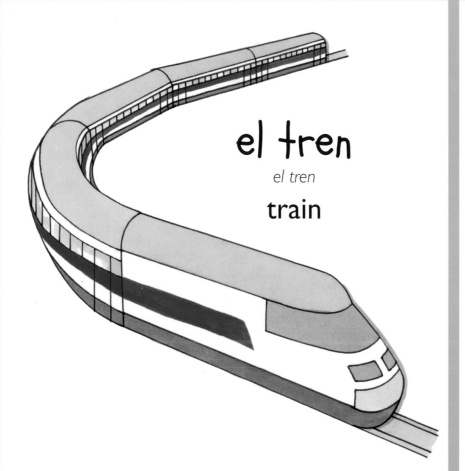

el tren

el tren

train

el barco

el barko

boat

el coche de bomberos

el kocheh deh bombair-oss

fire engine

el camión

el kamy-<u>on</u>

lorry

la excavadora

la eks-kaba-<u>dor</u>-a

digger

el tractor

el trak-<u>tor</u>

tractor

35

El tiempo Weather

el tee-empo

la lluvia

la yoo-beea

rain

el sol

el sol

sun

el viento

el bee-en-toh

wind

36

la niebla
la nee-aybla
fog

el hielo
el yeh-lo
ice

la nieve
la nee-eh-beh
snow

la nube

la <u>noo</u>-beh

cloud

la tormenta

la tor-<u>men</u>-ta

storm

el trueno

el troo<u>weh</u>-no

thunder

el relámpago

el rel-<u>lam</u>-pago

lightning

el arco iris

el arko <u>eer</u>-iss

rainbow

Los animales salvajes
Wild animals

loss anee-<u>mah</u>-less sal-<u>va</u>-hess

el león
el lay-<u>on</u>
lion

el hipopótamo
el eepo-<u>pot</u>-am-o
hippopotamus

el tigre

el <u>tee</u>-greh

tiger

el elefante

el eleh-<u>fan</u>-teh

elephant

el oso polar

el osso pol-<u>lar</u>

polar bear

la cebra

la theb-ra

zebra

el cocodrilo

el kokko-dree-lo

crocodile

el mono

el mon-o

monkey

el canguro

el kahn-<u>goo</u>-roh

kangaroo

la serpiente

la sairp-<u>yen</u>-teh

snake

la jirafa

la hee-<u>rah</u>-fa

giraffe

43

Vocabulario Word list

boca-boo-<u>lah</u>-reeo

Spanish/**español** – English/**inglés**
ess-pan-<u>yol</u>   *een-<u>gless</u>*

el abrigo coat
la abuela grandmother
el abuelo grandfather
amarillo yellow
los animales animals
el arco iris rainbow
el autobús bus
el avión aeroplane
azul blue
la bañera bath
el barco boat
la bicicleta bicycle
blanco white
el caballo horse
la cabra goat
los calcetines socks
la cama bed
el camión lorry
la camiseta T-shirt
el canguro kangaroo
la casa home
la cebra zebra
el cerdo pig
cinco five
el coche car
el coche de bomberos fire engine
el cocodrilo crocodile
los colores colours
la comida food
el conejo rabbit
cuatro four
diez ten
dos two
el elefante elephant
la excavadora digger
la falda skirt
la familia family

el frigorífico fridge
la fruta fruit
la gallina chicken
el gato cat
gris grey
el helado ice-cream
la hermana sister
el hermano brother
el hielo ice
el hipopótamo hippopotamus
el huevo egg
el jersey jumper
la jirafa giraffe
los juguetes toys
los lápices de colores crayons
la leche milk
el león lion
la lluvia rain
la madre mother
marrón brown
el mono monkey
morado purple
la moto motorbike
naranja orange
negro black
la niebla fog
la nieve snow
la nube cloud
nueve nine
los números numbers
ocho eight
el oso polar polar bear
la oveja sheep
el padre father
el pan bread
el pantalón trousers
los pantalones cortos shorts

el pato duck
la pelota ball
el perro dog
las piezas blocks
el pijama pyjamas
la puerta door
el queso cheese
el ratón mouse
el relámpago lightning
el reloj clock
rojo red
el rompecabezas jigsaw puzzle
la ropa clothes
rosa pink
seis six
la serpiente snake
siete seven
el sol sun
el sombrero hat
el tambor drum
el tiempo weather
el tigre tiger
la tormenta storm
el tractor tractor
el transporte transport
el tren train
tres three
el triciclo tricycle
el trueno thunder
uno one
la vaca cow
la ventana window
verde green
el vestido dress
el viento wind
los zapatos shoes

English/inglés – Spanish/español
een-gless — *ess-pan-yol*

aeroplane el avión
animals los animales
ball la pelota
bath la bañera
bed la cama
bicycle la bicicleta
black negro
blocks las piezas
blue azul
boat el barco
bread el pan
brother el hermano
brown marrón
bus el autobús
car el coche
cat el gato
cheese el queso
chicken la gallina
clock el reloj
clothes la ropa
cloud la nube
coat el abrigo
colours los colores
cow la vaca
crayons los lápices de colores
crocodile el cocodrilo
digger la excavadora
dog el perro
door la puerta
dress el vestido
drum el tambor
duck el pato
egg el huevo
eight ocho
elephant el elefante
family la familia
father el padre

fire engine el coche de bomberos
five cinco
fog la niebla
food la comida
four cuatro
fridge el frigorífico
fruit la fruta
giraffe la jirafa
goat la cabra
grandfather el abuelo
grandmother la abuela
green verde
grey gris
hat el sombrero
hippopotamus el hipopótamo
home la casa
horse el caballo
ice el hielo
ice-cream el helado
jigsaw puzzle el rompecabezas
jumper el jersey
kangaroo el canguro
lightning el relámpago
lion el león
lorry el camión
milk la leche
monkey el mono
mother la madre
motorbike la moto
mouse el ratón
nine nueve
numbers los números
one uno
orange naranja
pig el cerdo
pink rosa
polar bear el oso polar

purple morado
pyjamas el pijama
rabbit el conejo
rain la lluvia
rainbow el arco iris
red rojo
seven siete
sheep la oveja
shoes los zapatos
shorts los pantalones cortos
sister la hermana
six seis
skirt la falda
snake la serpiente
snow la nieve
socks los calcetines
storm la tormenta
sun el sol
ten diez
three tres
thunder el trueno
tiger el tigre
toys los juguetes
tractor el tractor
train el tren
transport el transporte
tricycle el triciclo
trousers el pantalón
T-shirt la camiseta
two dos
weather el tiempo
white blanco
wind el viento
window la ventana
yellow amarillo
zebra la cebra

45